D1259658

HOW DID IT HAPPEN?
THE HOLOCAUST

Sean Sheehan

LUCENT BOOKS
An imprint of Thomson Gale, a part of The Thomson Corporation

Detroit • New York • San Francisco • San Diego • New Haven, Conn.
Waterville, Maine • London • Munich

THOMSON

GALE

Produced by Arcturus Publishing Ltd
26/27 Bickels Yard
151–153 Bermondsey Street
London SE1 3HA

© 2005 Arcturus Publishing

Series concept: Alex Woolf
Editor: Rebecca Gerlings
Designer: Stonecastle Graphics
Picture researchers: Thomas Mitchell and
    Shelley Norohna

Picture credits:
All images copyright of Getty Images except for cover and
page 22, copyright of CORBIS; and pages 30 and 40, copyright of USHMM, Washington, D.C.

Thomson and Star Logo are trademarks and Gale and Lucent
Books are registered trademarks used herein under license.

For more information, contact
Lucent Books
27500 Drake Rd.
Farmington Hills, MI 48331-3535
Or you can visit our Internet site at http://www.gale.com

LIBRARY OF CONGRESS CATALOGING-IN-PUBLICATION DATA

Sheehan, Sean, 1951–
    The Holocaust / by Sean Sheehan.
        p. cm. — (How did it happen?)
    Includes bibliographical references and index.
    ISBN 1-59018-607-9 (hard cover : alk. paper)
    1. Holocaust, Jewish (1939–1945)—Juvenile
    literature. I. Title. II. Series.
    D804.34.S534 2005
    940.53'18—dc22
                                        2004024452

Printed in Singapore

Contents

1 The Roots of the Holocaust

T he Holocaust is the name given to the murder of 6 million Jews in Europe and to the attempt to eradicate Jewish culture during Nazi rule in Germany under Adolf Hitler.

The history of the Jewish people goes back 4,000 years in recorded time, their origins before then lying with nomadic peoples of Arabia. Jews were a part of the world's earliest civilization in Mesopotamia, and lived a seminomadic existence in what is now the Middle East. In territory where Palestinians and Israelis now live, they conquered an area that became a Jewish kingdom. By the beginning of the Christian era—2,000 years ago—about one in every ten people living in the Mediterranean region of the Middle East was Jewish.

As empires rose and fell in the Middle East, the Jews who lived there were subject to different rulers. As part of the Roman Empire, Jews lost their independent state and after a failed revolt in A.D. 70 they began to spread across many parts of Europe.

The Jews were just one of the many groups of people who migrated across the European continent. Their strong sense of a separate identity, however, kept them apart from other communities, and their own religion forbade them from living among non-Jews.

This carving is part of the Arch of Titus in Rome. It celebrates the conquest of the Jews by the Roman commander Titus, who became emperor in A.D. 79.

Christian Anti-Semitism

Christianity, which started as a minor offshoot of the Jewish religion, adopted a particularly hostile attitude toward the Jews. According to the Bible, it was Jews who called for Christ to be crucified, so it became common for Christians to label Jews as the "Christ-killers." The Jews' desire to live separately from their Christian neighbors made it easy to isolate them within fixed areas of towns, called ghettos. Outside of these areas Jews were often forced to wear a special badge, usually yellow, and prejudice against Jews became a deep-rooted aspect of many people's thinking. This prejudice was called anti-Semitism because Jews are classified as Semites, a word derived from the Greek *Shem*, the son of Noah in the Bible, from whom the Jews are traditionally supposed to be descended.

In 1096, violent attacks on Jews, called pogroms, took place in central Europe for the first time when up to 8,000 Jews were killed by Christian crusaders. In the twelfth century, a myth emerged that Jewish people ritually murdered Christian children in order to use their blood in the Passover religious festival. This myth became known as the "blood libel." Jews were also blamed for outbreaks of plague in Europe during this period. Plague, some said, was God's punishment of Christians for accepting Jews, the killers of Christ, into their society.

This anti-Semitic drawing from around the middle of the fourteenth century, depicting the Christian myth of the "blood libel," shows Jews collecting blood from Christian children.

Another source of Christian resentment against Jews lay in the Jewish practice of money lending. Officially, the Christian Church disapproved of the charging of interest for the lending of money. Although there were in fact Christian bankers, in popular thought the practice of money lending became associated with Jews only. Many trades and professions were forbidden to Jews, but money lending was not. This helped in the development, within Jewish communities, of a class of wealthy merchants during the Middle Ages. These Jewish merchants sometimes became a source of resentment, especially when it was convenient for Christian leaders to blame them for economic problems. This increased the isolation of Jews and, together with religious prejudice, led to the expulsions of Jews from western Europe.

These expulsions, along with massacres of Jews, began in the thirteenth century. Jews were expelled from England in 1290 and

France in 1306. In the fifteenth century, Jews were expelled from Spain and Portugal. Fleeing eastward into Italy and what is now Poland, they were finally welcomed for their education and financial competence.

Jews in Eastern Europe

By the sixteenth century, Jewish culture in Europe was centered in eastern Europe, in what is now Ukraine, Belorussia, Poland, and the Baltic countries. A strong Jewish community emerged, speaking a mixture of the local language and Hebrew, with its own literature and customs.

When Poland was split up in the eighteenth century, many of eastern Europe's Jews found themselves ruled as part of the Russian Empire. Here they were restricted as to where they could live, unlike the Jews from the western parts of Poland who were free to move into western towns and cities. In 1800, there were about 2 million Jews in Europe and, by 1900, this number had increased to 9 million. In most places, Jews enjoyed the same rights as other citizens, but in Russia they were subject to persecution and pogroms.

This illustration, from the late nineteenth century, shows Jews being kept against their will in the city of Kiev and reflects the persecution of Jews that was widespread in Russia at that time.

The Emergence of Modern Anti-Semitism

New ideas about the equality of citizens developed in the nineteenth century and led to the removal of ghettos and the extension of civil rights to Jewish people in most parts of Europe. In the twentieth century, however, Jewish culture in central and eastern Europe was very traditional, and Jewish communities tended to remain in separate areas of towns and cities. Despite this (except in the Russian-controlled areas of eastern Europe), there was more mixing of Jews with non-Jews. Jewish people could, and often did, become successful members of mainstream society.

Theories of Race

Although Jews were no longer persecuted for their minority religion, centuries of religious prejudice had left an enduring tradition of hatred for Jews. This hatred was fed by supposedly scientific ideas that were used to support racist beliefs about the natural superiority of white people. Such ideas, going back to the second half of the eighteenth century, developed as a part of European culture in the nineteenth century, and they lasted well into the following century. According to these theories, Semites, and the people of eastern Europe and

Russia—called Slavs—were inferior races, as were Africans and Asians. The race of white people who were the source of progress and civilization were called Aryans, and the Germans were seen by some as the purest Aryans. Ideas like these were put forward by a variety of scholars, including historians and biologists, and anti-Semites claimed that the Aryan race was in danger of being weakened by mixing with Jews. Such ideas were taken up by Hitler, the man who would become the leader of Germany in 1933.

Hitler and Anti-Semitism

Adolf Hitler, born in 1889 in Austria, was the son of a middle-class government officer. His father wanted him to be a businessman, but Hitler's only interests in school lay in drawing and gymnastics. He failed to complete his secondary education, and in his early adult years lived off the widow's pension that his mother received. Failing to get into art school, he moved to Vienna and lived in hostels, painting postcards that he sold on the street. He joined the German Army at the outbreak of World War I in 1914.

Adolf Hitler, pictured above in uniform during World War I, regarded Jews as responsible for the war. He believed they conspired against Germany after the war's end in 1918 when the country was defeated.

World War I ended in 1918 with the defeat of Germany, and the country was forced to accept the terms of the Treaty of Versailles. Under these terms, Germany lost some of its territory in Europe, as well as its colonies overseas. Its army was restricted in size, and massive fines had to be paid to the victorious countries as compensation. Anti-Semites claimed the harsh terms of the treaty were part of a Jewish conspiracy against Germany. German Jews were blamed for using their money to support the war against Germany and for not joining the army and fighting for their country.

Hitler accepted these anti-Semitic beliefs and found support for them in a document, called the *Protocols of the Elders of Zion*, which became well-known in the years after World War I. The document was a fake, but it was accepted by many who believed it was written by Jewish members of a group conspiring to conquer the world.

The *Protocols* claimed that Jews were behind the spread of Communist ideas and that these ideas would be used to destroy Christian culture. Many Communists were Jews and, when a Communist revolution took place in Russia in 1917, it was seen by anti-Semites as proof of a Jewish conspiracy.

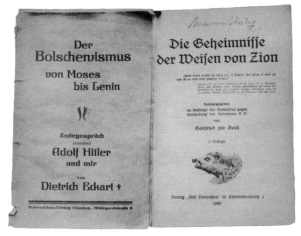

The Protocols of the Elders of Zion, a faked document, claimed to disclose secret plans by Jews to gain world domination.

In 1923, Germany's currency dramatically lost value and shops like this one were forced to close down.

Hitler, advertised in this poster as the speaker for a Nazi meeting in Munich in February 1925, became an accomplished public speaker who practiced the art of addressing large crowds and creating an emotional atmosphere.

Anti-Semites such as Hitler also found support for their prejudices in events in Germany after World War I. An elected government called the Weimar took power in Germany. Several members of the Weimar government were Jews, which added to the hatred of the government by anti-Semites, who blamed it for accepting the harsh terms of the Treaty of Versailles.

Jews led two attempts by Communist groups to take over the German government, in 1918 and 1919. The Communists wanted a government that would take over private companies, and this alarmed the business class of Germany. Anti-Semites could appeal to the business class by blaming Jews for the activities of Communists.

Nazi Ideas

After World War I, Hitler joined an anti-Semitic party. He soon gained influence within it and by 1920 had shaped it into the Nazi party.

In 1923, France invaded the Ruhr region of western Germany, taking most of the country's coal industries and steel mills. France's rationale for doing this was the Weimar government's failure to pay the $33 billion debt that Germany owed France as a result of the Treaty of Versailles. The loss of the Ruhr triggered massive inflation in Germany. The German currency, the deutsche mark, lost all its value, and thousands of businesses were forced to close.

Nazism took advantage of these economic problems by blaming Jews for what was happening, appealing to people who wanted a simple explanation for complicated problems. The Nazi party also became very anti-Communist, to attract the German business class and middle-class people who feared the possibility of a Communist government.

In the same year, the Nazi party led a public uprising against the Weimar government. Hitler organized a meeting and a march through the streets of Munich in the hope that people would rise up in support and declare him leader. He failed miserably in his attempt. However, his arrest and trial for treason did win him publicity, because he criticized in court the judge who sent him to prison and the trial was widely reported across Germany.

The Rise of Nazism

When Hitler emerged from prison in 1924, he found the Nazis with little or no support, and in the elections of 1928, the Nazis gained only 2.6 percent of the vote. Hitler began to reorganize the Nazi party, building support groups in rural areas, where he knew there was deep-seated racism. He created the Hitler Youth, a Nazi student organization, followed in 1928 by a Nazi doctors' group, a teachers' group, and also a cultural group that stressed German culture and language. All of these small organizations were aimed at picking up the support of different sections of society that felt unhappy with the government and the overall state of Germany. There was a worldwide economic depression,

Supporters of Hitler celebrate his arrival in the city of Nuremberg in 1933, the year he became chancellor of Germany.

with some 8 million people unemployed in Germany alone, and Hitler promised to deal with this problem. By assuring people that Communists would have no say in any future government, Nazism promised to end political divisions and restore to the German people a sense of pride in their country.

In the last two German elections before 1933, the Nazi party did not gain a majority of seats in the German parliament, or Reichstag, but they won more votes than any party since elections had begun in 1920. Because another small group of anti-Communists supported Hitler, he was made the political leader of Germany when he became chancellor in January 1933.

Nazi Laws

Once in power, Hitler moved swiftly to remove the democratic system of government. Laws were passed reducing the freedom of the press and banning public meetings. Anti-Jewish laws were introduced, designed to remove Jewish people from social and cultural life. Jews were banned from government service and the law. Jewish doctors and university teachers were restricted from working, and the number of Jewish students who could enroll in German schools and universities was also reduced. Books by Jewish writers were burned publicly, and all Jews who had been naturalized as German after 1918, about 100,000 people, lost their citizenship.

„WIDER DEN UNDEUTSCHEN GEIST"

This Nazi advertisement shows the first burning of books by Jewish and Communist writers, organized as a public event in Berlin within a few months of Hitler becoming chancellor.

TURNING POINT

The Enabling Law of 1933

Hitler held a general election in March 1933, hoping to finally win a majority of seats in the Reichstag. Although he gained 43.9 percent of the votes, this did not give him the overall majority that would allow him to pass whatever laws he wanted, so he proposed an Enabling Law that would give him the right to do this. When the Reichstag met to discuss this law on March 23, the eighty-one Communist members of the Reichstag had either been arrested or were blocked from entering the building. The law was passed by 441 votes to 94, ending democracy in Germany and making Hitler the country's dictator. Under the Enabling Law, Hitler was legally able to make anti-Semitic laws.

In 1933, the first concentration camps were set up. These were special prison camps where anyone the Nazis regarded as an enemy could be sent to be punished. The first prisoners were political opponents of the government who were, for the most part, Communists, Socialists, and trade union leaders.

On April 1, 1933, the Nazis proclaimed a boycott against Jewish shops and businesses that lasted for three days. Notices that read "Don't buy from Jews!" were posted on Jewish businesses.

Attacking Jews

Nazi laws brought the Jews under further attack. Jews were prohibited from marrying non-Jewish people—the Aryan race. The growing anti-Semitism led to Jewish homes and synagogues being attacked, often openly, by Nazi gangs. By 1938, one-third of Germany's 525,000 Jews had emigrated, many to the United States and Britain. Then, in October 1938, Hitler expelled from Germany 18,000 Jews who had been born in the Russian Empire but had lived for years in Germany. Their property was confiscated, and they were driven over the border into Poland and abandoned. The son of one of these families, living

TURNING POINT

Eliminating the weak

Part of the Nazi view of life was the idea that the weak and the handicapped were a disease in society. In May 1939, Hitler introduced a program of euthanasia—the "mercy killing" of severely ill or handicapped children. Five thousand children were killed in this way. A few months later, the program was extended to adults and included the mentally ill. By the time it stopped in August 1941, more than 70,000 people had been killed and a turning point had been reached. There had been little public protest over the killings so the Nazis had no reason to believe that anyone would object when the killing came to include Jews.

A worker clears the glass from a Jewish shop after the night of November 9, 1938. There was so much broken glass in the streets after the attacks that the destruction was given the name Kristallnacht, German for "night of broken glass."

in Paris, was so angered by the expulsion that he shot a German official living in the same city. This gave the Nazis an excuse to target Jews more violently than before. The attack became known as *Kristallnacht*, German for the "night of broken glass."

Kristallnacht

On November 9, 1938, Jewish synagogues, shops, and homes were attacked and burned, and the next morning, broken glass littered the streets. Many Jewish people died that night, and many thousands more were arrested and sent to the concentration camps. Within a month, a thousand of them had been murdered. Kristallnacht marked a turning point in the Nazi war against the Jews. The German public had tolerated the event and some had taken part in it.

More anti-Jewish laws were passed. They prevented Jews from owning or running any business; using sleeping or dining cars on trains; using public swimming pools or baths; attending schools, theaters, and cinemas; and staying in hotels. Jews were cut out completely from German social and economic life. An emigration office was set up to encourage Jews to leave Germany, and the emigration process was monitored to make sure that they did, in fact, leave the country.

HOW DID IT HAPPEN?

Were Nazis always anti-Semitic?

The Nazis pursued anti-Semitic policies, but they may not have always intended to act in this way. Historian Sarah Ann Gordon observes that "surprisingly few of the top Nazi leaders were virulent anti-Semites before 1925." Some historians claim that anti-Semitism for most Nazis—with the exception of Hitler— was just a way of gaining votes by appealing to people's prejudices. Where anti-Semitism was not strong, the Nazis did not pursue such ideas. Many historians, including Richard Overy, believe that anti-Semitism came to dominate Nazi policy only after Hitler gained power: "The entire system that emerged after 1933 was fundamentally anti-Semitic in its outlook, purpose and practices."

Sarah Ann Gordon, *Hitler, Germans and the "Jewish Question"* (Princeton, 1984); Richard Overy, *The Dictators* (Penguin, 2004)

During the night of November 9, 1938—Kristallnacht—more than 7,000 Jewish businesses such as this one were attacked and vandalized, nearly 100 Jews were killed, and thousands more were injured.

2 Starting the Holocaust

In 1938, the German Army occupied Austria and declared it to be a part of Germany. Austria's 185,000 Jews suddenly found themselves the victims of Nazi anti-Semitism. They were dismissed from government jobs, and their homes were robbed. Within a few months, nearly 70 percent of Austrian Jews had fled to countries willing to accept them as refugees.

Hitler was not content with the occupation of Austria. Nazi policies included the demand for what was called lebensraum ("living space") on the grounds that the Aryan race needed room to expand. World War II started when Hitler put this policy into effect by invading Poland, Germany's eastern neighbor, in September 1939. It was clear to Britain and France that Hitler wanted to control all of Europe, and they declared war on Germany to try to stop him.

The invasion of Poland placed nearly 2 million Polish Jews in the hands of the Nazis. Hitler was able to treat them as he wished and did not have to take into account public opinion, as he did in Germany. As German troops entered a Polish town, large numbers of Jews, along with non-Jews who might pose a threat to German control, were rounded up and murdered. In less than two months, 5,000 Jews and 10,000 non-Jews were killed.

The invasion of Poland and the start of war created the conditions that would allow the Holocaust to take place. As Hitler invaded and conquered more countries, it became possible to persecute all the Jews in countries under German control. Other countries that had already taken in Jewish refugees, and which were not themselves free of anti-Semitism, began to set limits on the numbers of Jews they were prepared to take in. With avenues of escape disappearing rapidly, the Jews of Europe were trapped. Hitler's persecution of Jews would develop into a system of mass murder so as to fulfill the Nazi goal of complete destruction of Jewish life and culture in Europe. The first stage in achieving this goal was the creation of ghettos.

Creating the Ghettos

The Warthegau province in the west of Poland was made a part of Germany, and all the Jews living there were driven out. Hitler's plan for all Jews in other parts of the country was to confine them in areas where they could be strictly controlled. These areas were called ghettos, and walls were built around them. The two largest ghettos were in the Polish cities of Warsaw—the capital—and Lodz.

VOICES FROM THE PAST

The hatred of Jews

Anti-Semitism was unleashed by the Nazis in Poland. This is revealed in the memory of a Polish Jew, captured after the invasion of his country, who recalls the attitude of a German guard when he was spotted resting on a cart:

"He made me get off the cart, aimed his rifle at me and bellowed: 'Du kannst laufen, Jude.' 'You can run, Jew.' He began pushing me towards those at the front . . . constantly threatening to shoot me, cutting my coat with his bayonet. When the German cavalry passed us he pushed me among the horses so that they should trample me."

Dan Cohn-Sherbok, *Understanding the Holocaust* (Cassell, 1999)

Following the German invasion of Poland in 1939, these Jewish men in the capital city of Warsaw were rounded up and escorted through the streets to a concentration camp.

VOICES FROM THE PAST

Isolating Jews

Some observers saw that the creation of the ghettos would lead to the Holocaust. An American journalist, William L. Shirer, was in Berlin in 1939, and he recorded in his diary on November 19 an announcement about the Warsaw ghetto:

"The Governor-general of occupied Poland, today decreed that the Jewish ghetto in Warsaw henceforth must be shut off from the rest of the capital by barricades and placed under sharp police control. He says the Jews are 'carriers of diseases and germs.' An American friend back from Warsaw tonight tells me the Nazi policy is simply to exterminate the Polish Jews. They are being herded into eastern Poland and forced to live in unheated shacks and robbed of any opportunity of earning bread and butter."

Martin Gilbert, *Never Again* (HarperCollins, 2000)

The sign in this Jewish part of Warsaw, where people are collecting water, reads "infected area." German forces put up such signs to insult and intimidate Jews.

Life in the ghettos was extremely harsh. Supplies of food were kept deliberately low by the Nazis, and in the second half of 1941, almost 30,000 Jews died of starvation in the Warsaw ghetto. Those capable of labor were rounded up and put to work building roads and camps for the German troops, returning to the ghetto at the end of each day. Within the ghettos, Jewish councils were set up to run everyday matters and carry out German demands for work parties.

Those people chosen, usually by the Nazis, to be members of the Jewish councils were faced with difficult choices. By cooperating with the Germans, they were helping to run the ghettos, but if they resisted the German demands, they could receive terrible punishment.

Life became even harsher when the Nazis began transporting to the ghettos Jews from other countries that had been conquered by Germany. This made them even more overcrowded, and whole families were squeezed into one room with little food, heat, or lighting and little or no sanitation. Jewish councils set up their own police forces, and sometimes they acted very harshly toward their own people. They forced some to join the work groups demanded by the Nazis and allowed rich people to escape these work groups by making payments. Those who were able to smuggle valuables into the ghetto had a better chance of survival. They could buy extra food on the black market or bribe their way out of a work assignment.

Life became a struggle for survival in the ghettos. People tried to trade what they owned to gain a little money that could be spent buying food.

Map legend:
- Einsatzgruppe A
- Einsatzgruppe B
- Einsatzgruppe C
- Einsatzgruppe D
- Frontline Dec. 1941
- Frontline Nov. 1942
- Greater Germany border Sept. 1939

Jews were driven out from Wartheland—the region of western Poland that was rechristened Warthegau when it became part of Germany—and the Einsatzgruppen swept eastward across eastern Europe, killing Jews and encouraging anti-Semitic murders in Ukraine, Belorussia, Lithuania, Latvia, and Estonia.

Invasion of Russia

As difficult as life was for Jews in the Polish ghetto, their chances of survival changed for the worse as the war took its course. Hitler decided to extend German power and conquer western Europe. In 1940, France, Belgium, Holland, Norway, Denmark, and Luxembourg fell to Nazi armies. This brought another million Jews under German control. Jews who had earlier fled Poland and Germany now found themselves trapped inside German-controlled territory. All Jews in the conquered countries were persecuted and gradually sent off to ghettos in Poland. The Nazis, who had once dreamed only of driving Jews out of Germany, now controlled the fate of approximately 4 million Jews.

In 1941, Germany invaded the Union of Soviet Socialist Republics (USSR). German troops advanced with speed into the USSR, and following behind them were the *Einsatzgruppen*. There were four of these special mobile murder squads, each made up of between 600 and 1,000 men. As each Russian town and village was taken, more Jews came under German control until, by 1942, another 2 million defenseless Jews were at the mercy of Nazi Germany.

TURNING POINT

Hatred unleashed

German troops were at first successful in their invasion of the USSR, and the Soviet Army was forced to retreat eastward. The Nazi murder squads found that in many areas no longer under Soviet control, the local people were willing to help round up and execute their Jewish neighbors. The German invasion unleashed anti-Semitic feelings in places like Ukraine, Belorussia, and the states of Latvia, Lithuania, and Estonia. The head of one murder squad, Colonel Karl Jaeger, reported that in Estonia, Latvia, and Lithuania his men had murdered 200,000 Jews and turned the remaining 34,000 into slaves. They had done so with the help of local volunteers, and Jaeger was full of praise for the volunteers' assistance.

Heinrich Himmler, in the center, was given complete control over German-occupied Poland, as well as organization of the Einsatzgruppen.

The Einsatzgruppen

In the invasion of the USSR, the job of the Einsatzgruppen—the murder squads—was to eliminate people seen as enemies of the Nazi state. Male Jews were the main victims but not the only ones. Anyone identified as a Communist official was to be murdered, as well as Gypsies and people regarded as more Asian than European. Nazism regarded Asians as another inferior race.

When the Einsatzgruppen moved into an area, they began by separating Jews worth keeping alive—the strong and healthy who could become slave labor—and drove the others into nearby woods. Jews were often forced to dig mass graves before being gunned down one at a time on the edge of the pit. The members of these murder squads were mostly German policemen, rather than soldiers, but the Einsatzgruppen worked closely with the army. They also encouraged local groups of anti-Semitic or anti-Communist people to organize their own mass killings.

This photograph, showing Nazi soldiers supervising the burial of murdered Polish Jews, was smuggled out of Germany to alert the world about the Holocaust.

VOICES FROM THE PAST

Mass murder

Hermann Grabe, a German builder who was a witness to
mass murder by the Einsatzgruppen, described seeing a large
ditch full of about a thousand bodies and the man carrying
out the executions:

*"He sat, legs swinging, on the edge of the ditch. He had an
automatic rifle resting on his knees. . . . The people, completely
naked, climbed down steps which had been cut into the clay
wall of the ditch, stumbled over the heads of those lying there
and stopped at the spot indicated. . . . They lay down on top of
the dead or wounded; some stroked those still living and spoke
quietly to them. Then I heard a series of rifle shots."*

Dan Cohn-Sherbok, *Understanding the Holocaust* (Cassell, 1999)

The Einsatzgruppen represented another stage in the progress of
the Holocaust. The mass killing of Jews in eastern Europe was the
first time that a systematic policy of mass murder was organized by the
Nazi government.

The "Final Solution"

The Einsatzgruppen proved to be a prelude to the Holocaust. The
original Nazi plan was to collect Jews into ghettos in Poland
and use them as slave labor that could be worked to death. After
the invasion of the USSR, it became obvious that there were too
many Jews to use in this way. One earlier idea had been to create
a place where they could be kept, and the island of Madagascar
had been proposed as a Jewish reservation. This also came to be seen
as unworkable.

The idea of what came to be called the "Final Solution," or
Endlösung, was decided upon by Nazi leaders sometime in the second
half of 1941. In the autumn of that year, Hitler gave authority for the
deportation of German and Austrian Jews to the ghettos in Poland. By
the beginning of November, approximately 20,000 Jews had been
deported and, to make room for them, non-German Jews were
murdered. A little earlier, around mid-August, the Einsatzgruppen
were instructed to start killing women and children as well as male
Jews. However, even then their systematic acts of mass murder could
not cope with numbers that went into millions. In his diary, on

TURNING POINT

The Wannsee Conference

In January 1942, a conference was held at Wannsee, outside Berlin, to explain the "Final Solution" to high-ranking Nazi officials who would organize and plan the genocide. An outline of the numbers of all Jews in Europe, including those in the neutral countries of Switzerland and Ireland, was presented to those present. It came to 11 million in total. Murdering Jews was the most important task, but other minorities, including Gypsies and homosexuals, were also to be eliminated. Notes of the meeting were copied and passed down to all the government departments that would play a part in the genocide.

On January 20, 1942, a secret meeting took place in this house at Wannsee, a Berlin suburb, to agree on arrangements for the final stages of the Holocaust.

December 13, Joseph Goebbels, a very high-ranking Nazi, wrote: "The World War is here, the extermination of the Jews must be the necessary consequence." The plan now was to be the complete physical elimination of every Jew in Europe.

The deliberate killing of such great numbers of people, something never attempted before, meant planning murder along the lines of a factory process. An industrial system of killing was developed, in much the same way that cars or cans were mass produced. It was decided that the use of poison gas would be the most efficient method. It had been used earlier in the euthanasia program, and now it would be extended to deal with the plan to kill millions. By the spring of 1942, work got underway to identify every Jew in Europe and, having identified them, deport them to a death camp in Poland where they could be murdered.

Josef Mengele, a German doctor, became the chief medical officer at the Auschwitz concentration camp in May 1943. He was known by inmates as the "Angel of Death" because he dressed in a spotlessly white medical coat and helped decide who should live or die.

HOW DID IT HAPPEN?

Were Jewish councils to blame?

Was it only the Germans who organized and made possible the Holocaust? Hannah Arendt, a German Jewish thinker, thought the Jewish councils in the ghettos made it easier to organize the Holocaust: "Jewish officials could be trusted to compile the lists of persons and of their property, to secure money from the deportees to defray the expenses of their deportation and extermination, to keep track of vacated apartments, to supply police forces, to help seize Jews and get them on trains." She believed that if the Jews had been less organized and cooperative, more of them would have survived.

Isaiah Trunk, however, in a study of Jewish councils, emphasized that "the Jews were forced to establish the councils, that individuals were forced to provide services for the Germans."

Michael R. Marrus, *The Holocaust in History* (Penguin, 1993)

3 The Death Camps

Between December 1941 and the summer of 1942, six death camps were set up in Poland. Two of them—Auschwitz and Majdanek—were labor and prison camps to which gas chambers were added. Three others, Belzec, Sobibor, and Treblinka, were specially built for the purpose of killing Jews as soon as they arrived. At these five camps, Jews were never told what was to happen to them. On arrival, they were informed that they would be given a shower but, instead of water, poison gas was released into the chambers where they were assembled.

This group of Soviet prisoners at Majdanek death camp were saved from the gas chamber when Soviet troops liberated the camp in July 1944. Altogether, about 200,000 people died at Majdanek.

VOICES FROM THE PAST

Burying the dead

Yakov Grojanowski, a Jew who was not gassed on arrival at Chelmno, was forced to assist with the burial of the corpses. He remembers January 12, 1942:

"That afternoon the work lasted till six. Nine vans, each of sixty Jews from Klodawa, were buried; five hundred from Klodawa in all. My friend Getzel Chrzastowski screamed terribly for a moment when he recognized his fourteen-year-old son, who had just been thrown into the ditch. We had to stop him, too, from begging the Germans to shoot him."

Martin Gilbert, *Never Again* (HarperCollins, 2000)

The six major Nazi death camps were located in eastern Poland and were usually close to railway lines so that victims could be easily transported to them in large numbers.

The sixth death camp, Chelmno, was different in that it relied on the use of specially adapted vans that channeled the poisonous exhaust fumes back inside the vans themselves. Jews inside the van were killed by the fumes as they were being driven into a nearby forest. The only Jews not killed were those used for burying the dead in the forest. The gassing of about 400,000 people started at Chelmno in December 1941.

Auschwitz

Once Poland's Jews had been murdered, Auschwitz became the main killing center for Europe's remaining Jews. Gypsies and homosexuals were also sent to Auschwitz to be killed. The camp was built on an area of farmland, around nineteen square miles in area, outside the town of Oswiecim, which in German became Auschwitz.

The original camp was built in 1940 and was designated a work camp where Jews and political prisoners were brought to be detained. Some of these died while in the camp, but that was not its primary purpose. In 1941, a second camp was begun, called Birkenau after the name of the nearby village, and this became the main death factory as well as a work camp. There were three gas chambers at Birkenau capable of holding over 1,000 people. A third camp was a large slave labor factory run by a large German chemical company called I.G. Farben. There were lots of smaller work camps, including a shoe factory, in the surrounding area that became part of the main Auschwitz system.

The location of Auschwitz was chosen by the Nazis because of railway links that connected it with other parts of Europe. When a trainload of victims arrived at Auschwitz, the victims were ordered off and formed into two lines. There were usually two doctors on the platform, whose job was to help divide the new arrivals into able-bodied younger men and women—who could become slave labor—and older men and women, and children. These people, told they would be given a shower, were taken instead to the gas chambers and were dead within a few hours of arrival at the camp. Their bodies were burned and the ashes dumped.

In the years that Auschwitz operated, between 40,000 and 120,000 slave laborers lived in 200 wooden huts in the Birkenau camp. They were controlled by around 7,000 German guards. The process of killing at Birkenau became as streamlined as possible and, by 1944,

British troops who liberated the Bergen-Belsen concentration camp in Germany in April 1945 found thousands of unburied dead and mass graves filled with 40,000 bodies.

VOICES FROM THE PAST

"We didn't believe it"

Lilli Kopecky was a Jew from Slovakia who was deported to Auschwitz. Selected for work rather than immediate death, she remembers how Jews could not always believe what was happening at Auschwitz:

"*I recall a Dutch Jew asking angrily, 'Where is my wife? Where are my children?' The Jews in the barracks said to him, 'Look at the chimney [of the gas chamber]. They are up there.' But the Dutch Jew cursed them. . . . This is the greatest strength of the whole crime, its unbelievability. When we came to Auschwitz, we smelt the sweet smell. They said to us: 'There the people are gassed, three kilometres over there.' We didn't believe it.*"

Martin Gilbert, *Never Again* (HarperCollins, 2000)

Of these Jews arriving at Auschwitz (bearing the yellow star that Nazis ordered to be sewn onto their coats as a mark of their Jewish identity), only some escaped immediate death in the camp's gas chambers.

VOICES FROM THE PAST

The work of a Treblinka guard

Willi Mentz, an SS guard at the Treblinka death camp,
had the job of shooting those who were too weak to walk
to a gas chamber. He describes his activities:

*"There were always some ill and frail people on these
[train] transports. . . . These people would be taken to the
hospital and stood or laid down at the edge of the grave. When
no more ill or wounded were expected it was my job to shoot
these people. I did this by shooting them in the neck with a 9-
mm pistol. They then collapsed or fell to one side and were
carried down into the grave by the two hospital work-Jews."*

Claude Lanzmann, *Shoah: The Complete Text of the Acclaimed
Holocaust Film* (Da Capo, 1995)

This member of the
Sonderkommando, with the
grim task of managing a bone-
crunching machine at a death
camp, was probably later shot
to prevent him from revealing
what he had been forced to do.

chambers after gassing and, equipped
with rubber shoes and water hoses,
washed down the bodies to make
them easier to handle. They tied straps
around the corpses and dragged them
toward the elevators that carried the
bodies up to the crematoriums. Here,
Jewish dentists were waiting to pull
out any gold teeth before the corpses
were fed into the giant ovens. Most
members of the Sonderkommando
were killed themselves after a few
months of work, when they had
become too weak to be of any use.

Transport to the Camps

The careful planning that went into the management of the death
camps was also applied to the task of organizing the transport of
victims to the camps. The first transports of Jews from Germany,
Czechoslovakia, and Austria took place from 1939 to 1942. Jews
were charged a fee for the cost of their transport, and they were
allowed to bring their belongings and food for the journey. Most of
these Jews went to the ghettos of Poland, but some arrived in
Auschwitz, fully believing that they were being resettled in the east.

colored triangle on their clothing to signify their status in the camp. A red triangle was for political prisoners, ordinary criminals wore a green one, homosexuals a pink one, and Jews a yellow triangle.

Many German companies and businesses made use of the slave labor that was available at the concentration camps and at some of the death camps. Outside Dachau, one of the original concentration camps inside Germany, over fifty companies built plants where the prisoners could be put to work. Many ordinary Germans also benefited from the plight of Jews, because when a Jewish family went off to the ghetto, their home or their job or their business would become available for a non-Jewish family to take over. There were always people in Nazi-occupied Europe who were willing to do this, and they knew they were profiting at the expense of Jews, even if they did not always know what was happening to those who were rounded up and taken away.

Personal items of any value, like the thousands of wedding rings photographed here after their discovery in a cave near the Buchenwald camp in 1945, were taken from Jews arriving at the concentration and death camps.

HOW DID IT HAPPEN?

How anti-Semitic were the Germans?

In his 1996 book, *Hitler's Willing Executioners*, author David Goldhagen claimed that it was easy for Hitler to bring about the Holocaust because of the preexisting "eliminationist anti-Semitism of the German people, which Hitler essentially unleashed." Goldhagen claimed that most Germans were so anti-Semitic that they were willing to cooperate in the Holocaust.

However, historians say that Goldhagen's explanation of the Holocaust is not only simple but, in its own way, racist because of the way it blames ordinary Germans. Historians have pointed out that many other ethnic and religious groups were murdered in the Holocaust and that in 1933 more than half the German population did not vote for the Nazis.

David Goldhagen, *Hitler's Willing Executioners* (Abacus, 1996)

4 Resisting the Holocaust

Helping Jews hide or escape was risky because anyone who did so could be killed by the authorities. Despite this, many people risked their lives to help Jewish people, and they did so for many reasons. Sometimes it was because they knew the Nazis would murder the Jews or because rescuing a Jewish family was one way of fighting Germany, and sometimes it was because Jewish people bribed them to help. In France, an underground movement smuggled Jews out of the country, and in Holland there were riots when the first Jewish deportations began. In Denmark, the entire Jewish population was rescued in a nationwide effort the day before the transports to the camps were to begin. In Berlin, large numbers of Jews survived the war, hidden by their friends or disguised as Aryans.

Even some of Germany's allies resisted giving up their Jews. In Italy and Hungary, both allies, deportations did not begin until 1943. Hungary took in many refugees from Czechoslovakia, Poland, and Germany. In Bulgaria, another German ally, ordinary people protested and stopped the transportation of Jews. Norway saved about half its Jewish population by ferrying Jewish citizens to neutral Sweden, and Finland simply refused to give up its Jews. China, and even Japan, also took in Jewish refugees.

Jewish people in Britain, the United States, and other countries found visas and work permits for their relatives. Jewish organizations sent cash and, for as long as it was possible, found new homes for refugees.

Resistance and Revolts

Many Jews could not rely on anyone to help them, and they took their own measures to resist and survive the Holocaust. In many of the ghettos, small groups of people decided to form resistance groups, even though discovery would almost certainly lead not only to their own deaths but to the deaths of their families and coworkers.

In most ghettos, resistance fighters were considered reckless and dangerous to the community, as illustrated by an incident in the ghetto of Vilna in Lithuania. A resistance group developed there after more than half of the ghetto's 57,000 Jews had been executed. The German in charge demanded that the Jewish council hand over the resistance leader, and the head of the council agreed to do so. He may have sincerely thought this was the best way to protect the lives of the majority in the ghetto. Many Jews in ghettos wanted to believe that if they kept working they would not be killed and would somehow survive the Holocaust. This, though, is not what usually happened. Shortly after the council in Vilna had sacrificed the resistance leader, the Nazis killed all the Jews who had been living there.

Sometimes, a whole ghetto acted together to resist the Nazis. In Tuczn, Poland, in 1942, the ghetto inmates were told to assemble at the gates of the ghetto the next morning. They knew that this meant

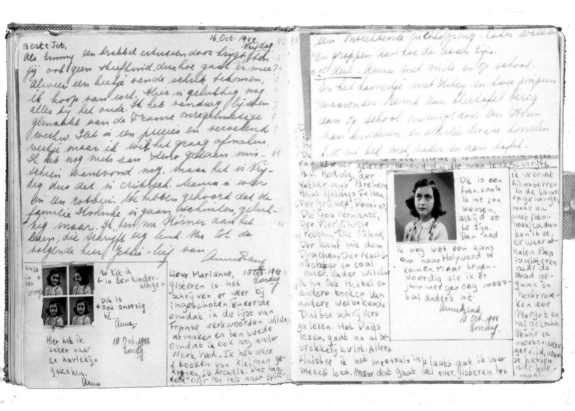

they would be transported to a death camp. Instead of meekly waiting to be transported, they began to burn the ghetto, destroying the factories and anything that might be useful to the Germans. In the confusion, about 2,000 people escaped into the woods, though few of them survived to the end of the war.

In 1942, an estimated 40,000 Jews escaped from ghettos and fled into local forests. It was very difficult to survive without food, and although some Polish villagers helped the escapees, many betrayed them in return for a small reward. However, some Jews preferred to die in the act of resisting rather than go quietly to a death camp.

Pages from the diary of Anne Frank tell of the Jewish girl's life with her family while she was kept hidden in a house in Amsterdam for four years. The family was betrayed in August 1944, and Anne was sent to the Bergen-Belsen camp, where she died.

VOICES FROM THE PAST

Fighting back

Members of a Jewish self-defense organization in the Bialystok ghetto in Poland called for support from others living in the ghetto. The following is part of their appeal:

"Do not go willingly to death! Fight for life to the last breath. Greet our murderers with teeth and claws, with axe and knife, hydrochloric acid and iron crowbars. Make the enemy pay for blood with blood, for death with death! Will you hide in mouse-holes when they drag out your dear ones to dishonour and death?!"

Martin Gilbert, *Never Again* (HarperCollins, 2000)

Two Jewish resistance fighters are captured by German soldiers after the uprising in the Warsaw ghetto in April 1943. The uprising took place as a symbolic act of defiance, because those fighting knew they could not succeed.

Warsaw Ghetto Uprising

The huge Warsaw ghetto housed many young people who wanted to resist what was happening to them. This led to the largest act of armed resistance by Jews in a ghetto.

Jews inside the Warsaw ghetto formed links with resistance groups in the city and bided their time, not wanting to bring down punishments on the other ghetto inmates. Over the months, the resistance group managed to obtain a few handguns and homemade hand grenades. In January 1943, some members of the resistance group were selected for one of the many deportations, and the others decided that the time was right to fight the Germans. Most of the resistance fighters were easily cut down by German automatic weapons, but the few survivors barricaded themselves inside a building. It took three days for the Germans to bring the rebellion under control, and in that time twelve German soldiers were killed.

The ghetto returned to its normal state until the following April. In the intervening months those resistance members who had survived began building hiding places and routes through the sewers in the hope that when the final battle came, some unarmed people

An injured woman is carried away after the failure of the second Warsaw uprising in 1944, which lasted for sixty-three days and involved about 35,000 Polish men and women.

The first Warsaw uprising was crushed by a force of some 3,000 Germans using artillery to blow up buildings where Jews were sheltering. This photograph was taken after the uprising.

TURNING POINT

Making a choice

In December 1942, U.S. president Franklin D. Roosevelt was told about the death camps in Poland. Britain had been given similar information months earlier. Later, in 1944, the United States and Britain occupied part of Italy and were able to bomb targets in Poland. The I.G. Farben factory at Auschwitz was bombed, but not the railway lines into Auschwitz or the gas chambers. At the time, Hungarian Jews were being gassed, and bombing Auschwitz might have saved them until the Russians arrived to liberate the camp. The decision not to bomb Auschwitz was a turning point in the war, in that it made it clear that the priority was the military defeat of Germany. The suffering of civilians in eastern Europe was not a priority for the American and British leaders. They could, however, argue that defeating Germany militarily was the best way to end the Holocaust.

HOW DID IT HAPPEN?

How much resistance was there?

One Jewish historian, Raul Hilberg, argues that because Jews lacked a tradition of self-defense, there was no significant armed resistance: "The reaction pattern of the Jew is determined by almost complete lack of resistance. The Jews attempted to tame the Germans as one would attempt to tame a wild beast."

Yehuda Bauer, another Jewish historian, comes to a different conclusion and gives an account of what he believes counted as acts of resistance against the Holocaust: "It includes smuggling food into the ghetto, mutual self-sacrifice within the family to avoid starvation or worse; cultural, educational, religious or political activities taken to strengthen morale. The work of doctors, nurses, and educators to consciously maintain health and moral fibre to enable individual and group survival; and of course armed rebellion."

Raul Hilberg, *The Destruction of the European Jews* (Quadrangle, 1961); Yehuda Bauer, *Rethinking the Holocaust* (Yale University Press, 2001)

might escape to safety. They had little hope for their own survival. In April, when rumors began to spread that the Nazis were planning to remove everyone from the ghetto to the death camps, the uprising began. Impressed by the strength of the previous attempt, the Polish underground had supplied the resistance leaders with two automatic weapons, rifles, and about 500 handguns. The resistance movement added their own gasoline bombs and homemade hand grenades. The Germans were well armed with tanks and they outnumbered the rebels two to one. Yet on the first day, the Germans were driven out of the ghetto, their weapons taken, and twelve were killed.

The Warsaw ghetto uprising lasted for a month. The Germans stayed outside the ghetto and fired mortar shells inside. In the chaos, several thousand people escaped from the ghetto and remained hidden in the city for the duration of the war. The resistance fighters fought to their deaths. Many thousands of people died in the onslaught, and the following September the ghetto was razed.

5 The End of the Holocaust

Prisoners in death camps eventually began to realize that they had a chance to escape and wait for the war to end. In August 1943, at the Treblinka death camp, fifteen guards were killed in a breakout that enabled 150 prisoners to escape, although some were hunted down and shot. In October of the same year, a planned revolt at the Sobibor death camp allowed 300 prisoners to escape. It is estimated that about 60 of them survived the war.

In the same month, a revolt by the Sonderkommando at Auschwitz led to the destruction of one of the crematoriums, but nearly all the 700 rebels were shot by prison guards. Explosives used by the rebels in the revolt were smuggled out by women working in a nearby explosives factory to Roza Robota inside Auschwitz. Robota was tortured after the revolt failed and was hanged on January 5, 1945.

Pictured here—second row from bottom and fifth from the left— is Roza Robota (1921–1945), a member of a Jewish resistance group in Auschwitz. Robota was tortured by the authorities after the failure of a revolt she helped organize.

Defeating Nazism

By 1943, many of the ghettos of eastern Europe had been emptied as their populations were dispatched by train to the death camps. Some of the camps themselves were being taken apart and the evidence of what they did being destroyed. Most of Europe's Jews were dead or in hiding. Also, by early 1944, it was becoming obvious that Germany

TURNING POINT

Defeated by Russia

In July 1943, the greatest tank battle of all time was waged in Kursk, in Russia. German troops were stretched across long lines and a successful invasion of the USSR depended on a victory at Kursk. The USSR, however, had finally got its war machine into operation and was on the offensive. Although thousands of troops died on both sides, the battle marked a decisive turning point in World War II. Hitler's troops began to retreat toward Germany, with the Soviet Army behind them. Soon after, Soviet troops reached Poland and ended the Holocaust.

could not win the war. The countries opposing Germany were known as the Allies and two of them, the United States and Britain, were about to invade northern France, while the USSR was ready to advance westward toward Poland. It was only a matter of time before Soviet troops fought their way into Germany. In June 1944, the Allies launched their D-day offensive, and by September, about 2 million Allied troops were fighting their way across France and into Germany.

Hitler's armies were sandwiched between two advancing forces. The Soviet Army was advancing from the east, while American and British forces were moving in from the west. Massive air attacks on German cities were taking place at the same time. The Nazis, however, chose to speed up the mass murder of Jews, rather than suspend the Holocaust so that Germany could concentrate on military matters.

These Hungarian Jews are leaving a railway boxcar after its arrival at Auschwitz in May 1944, having been transported from ghettos. Any who tried to resist were shot down in the station.

The Holocaust Continues

The Holocaust continued even as Russian troops were fighting their way into Hungary. In May 1944, the Nazis began emptying the country's ghettos, forcing their occupants onto trains to take them to Auschwitz, which was one of the death camps that remained. These trains could have been used to transport retreating German troops from Russia. Instead, in a period of about eight weeks, they were used to make sure that 400,000 Hungarian Jews were gassed at Auschwitz.

A British soldier in September 1945 examines the incinerator used to cremate the corpses of those who died at the Bergen-Belsen concentration camp in Germany. Of the 38,500 who remained alive when the camp was liberated in 1945, approximately 28,000 died soon afterwards from disease.

VOICES FROM THE PAST

Leaving evidence

Some Jewish prisoners in the camps tried to preserve evidence of the Holocaust, as if they knew people would find it difficult to believe what had taken place. The following note, written by a member of the Sonderkommando, and buried at Auschwitz in 1944, was discovered after the war:

"Dear finder, search everywhere, in every inch of soil. Dozens of documents are buried under it, mine and those of other persons, which will throw light on everything that was happening here. Great quantities of teeth are also buried here. It was we, the Kommando workers, who expressly have strewn them all over the terrain, as many as we could, so that the world should find material traces of the millions of murdered people."

Martin Gilbert, *Never Again* (HarperCollins, 2000)

Closing the Camps

The death camps did not all close down at the same time, but they gradually ceased to operate as it became obvious that Soviet forces would advance toward Poland. Belzec had closed down as early as December 1942, by which time most of Poland's Jews were dead. The Treblinka and Sobibor camps were dismantled by the Nazis toward the end of 1943 and, by July 1944, a resistance group had taken over the Majdanek camp. Auschwitz continued operating until October 1944, although it was January 1945 before the Germans left and forced the remaining 60,000 prisoners to march through the winter into Germany. As many as a third died along the way before the survivors were abandoned at the Bergen-Belsen concentration camp in Germany.

Two rows of Nazis sit in front of guards in a courtroom at the International War Crimes Tribunal that took place in Nuremberg, Germany, between November 1945 and October 1946.

VOICES FROM THE PAST

Will you speak out?

Different lessons can be learned from the Holocaust, and one of them is the importance of defending the rights of groups who are picked on and unfairly blamed for particular events. Martin Niemöller, a German imprisoned by the Nazis, wrote these words in 1946:

First they came for the socialists,
and I did not speak out—
because I was not a socialist.

Then they came for the trade unionists,
and I did not speak out—
because I was not a trade unionist.

Then they came for the Jews,
and I did not speak out—
because I was not a Jew.

Then they came for me,
and there was no one left
to speak out for me.

The Jewish Museum in Berlin, completed in 1999, was planned around an empty central space, a reminder of the city's Jews who either fled Berlin or died in the Nazi concentration and death camps.

Surviving the Holocaust

Those who had survived the Holocaust also had to survive the life that lay ahead of them. They faced a future in which their families, homes, and communities had been wiped out. They found themselves moved into displaced persons camps where they were still prisoners. Some who struggled back to their homes in eastern Europe were murdered on arrival by anti-Semitic groups. In Poland alone, about 1,000 Jewish people were murdered between 1945 and 1947. About a million Jews had stayed alive in the Nazi-occupied states of Europe. Most of them looked to the United States and to Palestine as places where they could go to try to build new lives.

For more than fifty years, Jewish groups had been campaigning for the creation of a Jewish state in Palestine. After 1945, with the war over and thousands of Jewish refugees in Europe with nowhere to go,

pressure began to mount on the British, who administered Palestine, to allow Jewish settlers in. In 1948, Britain withdrew from Palestine, and the United Nations passed a resolution dividing Palestine and creating the new state of Israel. This led to war between Israel and neighboring states, and hundreds of thousands of Arabs who had been living in what was now Israel became displaced persons cut off from their land.

People light candles in June 2004 during an opening ceremony of the museum and memorial monument in Belzec, one of the main Nazi death camps. There, an estimated 600,000 died. Only two people are known to have succeeded in escaping from the camp.

HOW DID IT HAPPEN?

Was justice done?

Over twenty Nazi leaders were put on trial at Nuremberg in Germany in October 1945, and most of them were found guilty. Several of them were hanged and others went to prison.

Historians, however, have questioned the extent to which this represented justice for the victims of the Holocaust. Those found guilty represented a tiny number compared to the many thousands of people who took part in the murder of Jews and other minorities. Historian Tim Cole points out that the murderous targeting of Jews itself "received scant attention in a trial more concerned with crimes against peace, war crimes and crimes against humanity."

Tim Cole, *Images of the Holocaust* (Duckworth, 1999)

Holocaust Time Line

1215 European Jews forced to wear distinctive clothing to identify them as Jews

1290 Jews expelled from England

1306 Jews expelled from France

1881–1882 Pogroms against Jews take place in Russia and Ukraine

1889 Adolf Hitler born

1919 The Treaty of Versailles punishes Germany for World War I with fines and the loss of territory

1929 Anti-Semitic groups formed throughout Germany by Hitler's Nazi party

1933 Hitler made chancellor of Germany

1935 Nuremberg laws deny German citizenship to Jews and take away their political rights

1938 During Kristallnacht, "the night of broken glass," Jewish synagogues and other buildings were vandalized throughout Germany and Jewish people attacked and killed

1939

September: World War II begins

November: All Jews in Nazi-occupied Europe forced to wear a yellow Star of David on their clothes

December: Jewish males, aged fourteen to sixty, required for forced labor in labor camps in Poland

1940 Jews are deported to the Warsaw ghetto

1941

June: Germany invades the USSR

September: Experiments on the gassing of prisoners begin at Auschwitz

October: The deportation of Jews to eastern Poland gets underway

December: The gassing of Jews begins at Chelmno death camp

1942

January: Wannsee Conference confirms plans for the mass murder of Jews

March: Transports of prisoners begin to the camps of Majdanek, Sobibor, Belzec, and Treblinka

May: Gassing on a large scale in operation at Auschwitz

1943

January: German forces surrender to Soviet Army in Russia

April: Gassing at Chelmno comes to an end

August: Gassing at Treblinka comes to an end

1944

May: Deportations of Hungarian Jews to Auschwitz begins

June: Allies land in northern France on D-day; Soviet armies advance westward toward Germany

October: Gassings at Auschwitz come to an end

1945

January: Soviet troops reach Auschwitz

May: Germany surrenders to the Allies

October: Nuremberg trials begin

1948 State of Israel established

Glossary

Allies Countries at war against Germany in World War II.

anti-Semitism Prejudice against Jews.

Aryan The Nazi term for white-skinned Europeans, not of Jewish, Slav, or Gypsy descent.

chancellor The head of the German government.

communism The belief that there should be no privately owned property, and that an economic system need not just be based on profit making.

concentration camps Large-scale prison and work camps, where prisoners would be worked to death.

crusaders Medieval soldiers who tried to recapture the Holy Land in the Middle East from the Muslims.

euthanasia In Nazi terms, the killing of people believed to be of no value to society.

"Final Solution" The Nazi term for the complete extermination of Jews across Europe.

genocide The deliberate attempt to kill a people or a nation.

Holocaust The term used to refer to the murder of 6 million Jews and smaller minority groups by the Nazis.

Mesopotamia Region of the Middle East, now Iraq.

Middle Ages Period of European history between the fall of the Roman Empire in 476 and around the middle of the fifteenth century.

Nazi party Short for *Nationalsozialistische Deutsche Arbeiterpartei*, National Socialist German Workers' Party, led by Hitler between 1933 and 1945.

nomadic Not living in one fixed place.

Slav People in central and eastern Europe, including Russians, Poles, and Hungarians.

USSR The abbreviation for the Union of Soviet Socialist Republics, dominated by Russia, which came to an end in the late 1980s.

For Further Information

Books:

Altman, Linda Jacobs. *Hitler's Rise to Power and the Holocaust*. Berkeley Heights, NJ: Enslow, 2003.

Frank, Anne. *The Diary of a Young Girl (The Definitive Edition)*. New York: Doubleday, 1995.

Grant, R.G. *The Holocaust*. Austin, TX: Raintree Steck-Vaughn, 1998.

Lawton, Clive. *Auschwitz: Story of a Nazi Death Camp*. Cambridge, MA: Candlewick Press, 2002.

Lawton, Clive. *The Story of the Holocaust*. New York: Franklin Watts, 1999.

Levy, Patricia. *Holocaust*. North Mankato, MN: Smart Apple Media, 2003.

Levy, Patricia M. *Holocaust Causes*. Chicago: Raintree, 2002.

Sheehan, Sean. *Death Camps*. Chicago: Raintree, 2002.

Shuter, Jane. *Aftermath of the Holocaust*. Chicago: Heinemann, 2003.

Web Sites

The Beth Shalom Holocaust Web Centre (www.bethshalom.com).

The Holocaust Centre, Beth Shalom (www.holocaustcentre.net).

The Holocaust History Project (www.holocaust-history.org).

Remember.org (www.remember.org).

Survivors of the Shoah Visual History Foundation (www.vhf.org)

United States Holocaust Memorial Museum (www.ushmm.org).

Index Page numbers in **bold** indicate photographs